Fake Your Way as an *Intentist*

Intentism for Beginners

Vittorio Pelosi

Intentism Publishing House

First published in Great Britain in 2018 by Intentism Publishing House.

Preface

The idea for this book grew out of a series of ten talks entitled 'Introducing Intentism' that can now be found on Youtube. The talks have been edited and a substantial amount of extra material has been added.

We hope that you will find the material engaging and thought-provoking. One final note: Vittorio Pelosi is currently engaged in writing a further work that goes into the movement's ideas and the complexities that surround them in much more detail and depth. So, if you decide to go beyond 'faking' your way as an Intentist, look out for it!

Contents

PART ONE – *INTENTISM AND*

ITS HISTORICAL CONTEXT

WHAT is Intentism?

Intentism is an international arts movement. It is comprised of fine artists, poets, writers, musicians, actors and philosophers from all over the world. At present it is one of the fastest growing art movements in the UK.

WHAT do Intentists do?

*The name **Intentism** is a response to the debate around authorial intent. Does it matter what the speaker/artist/author/ is intending what he or she says, paints or writes? Intentism maintains that the meaning of the work is the imperfect outworking of intention. Intentists create literary, visual and musical art to celebrate the importance of intention.*

Intentists believe that intention can often affect the way we view our experiences. Take a look at these two pairs of analogous events: After a violent altercation two men in Glasgow run over a thirty-nine year old man, leaving him for dead; an OAP fails to see a pedestrian and knocks him down. Secondly, a man incensed over unrequited love tracks down the object of his desires and shoots her dead; a woman from Cape Girardeau shoots and kills her attacker during an attempted rape. All tragic events, but should they be treated as equally *terrible*? In law, distinctions are made based on the perpetrator's intentions.

1. Intention... *What's all the fuss?*

Like our understanding of ethics and law, it is the belief of the new international movement 'Intentism' that intentions matter in the arts too.

Picture in the frame above an artwork of your own: *Is it a painting? A sculpture? An installation? What if viewers thought your work were **racist?***

*For them, your work means that white people are the master race and they are shocked and offended. As the creator, do you have the authority to tell these viewers that they are wrong? Can your work mean different things to different people? Can it mean anything? But if it means anything, it has the possibility of meaning everything. The result? It arguably means **nothing**. Your art is silent. You have no voice.*

Conversely, Intentism believes that 'All meaning is the imperfect outworking of intention.'

> Intentism
>
> All meaning is the imperfect outworking of intention

Intentism's central belief may seem uncontroversial; however, this theory is commonly rejected based on arguments which call into question such thinking as: Am I aware of all my reasons for what I do? Might I not subconsciously disclose Freudian Slips? What about *what* I communicate? As a literate person won't the clarity of my words or art speak for themselves, regardless of my intentions? Furthermore, do all readers approach the same work identically? Each time a couple says 'This is *our* song' doesn't the ballad acquire a new meaning?

To many, these questions expose Intentionalism in the arts as an obvious fallacy.

Intentionalism

The theory that all literary wor[k] should be judged by the author's intentions.

Not so, say the Intentists. This debate has raged in different guises over the centuries for a reason. It hits to the heart at what sets us apart from other animals. How do we communicate? *Can* we communicate?

Fake Your Way as an Intentist will give reasons why believing creative meaning is the outworking of intention frees up both the artwork and the artist.

This book will firstly look at the theory of what really goes on when we create something. Secondly, it will look at how grounding meaning as the 'imperfect outworking of intention' actually liberates the work, and lastly this book will look at some examples of Intentist art.

1. <u>How did we get to such a place?</u>
i) <u>Four Prominent Thinkers</u>

Today we are told that as we have innumerable influences on our decision-making processes, both conscious and unconscious, we really are not able to say what a work means. Moreover, since each viewer comes to a work with a different background, the work will mean different things to different people.

Let's begin by very briefly mentioning some of the leading thinkers that have shaped the arguments and then we will trace what socio-political factors had impact.

<u>Gadamer, Derrida and Barthes</u>

During the Romanticism of the early 18th century the author was a central figure in hermeneutics. Scholars would seek out the 'genius' behind the work. However, the 20th century saw a monumental change in approach. Much of it was shaped by the following men.

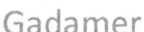
Gadamer

Firstly, German Continental philosopher, Hans Georg Gadamer, 1900- 2002, author of 'Art and Method' wrote about, 'The effective history of the work.' This is to say that a text or a piece of art may be seen by peoples of different cultures and times. Different generations and peoples may see the work differently. In the art world, this unique baggage a viewer brings to the work has also been termed the 'period eye.'

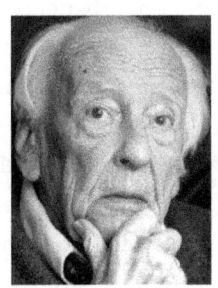
Meaning continually changes.

For example, is 'The Wonderful Wizard of Oz' about the arguments surrounding the Gold Standard in America, or a children's fantasy? To

Gadamer, these are not various reader's associations, but different meanings for different audiences.

Influenced by German philosopher Martin Heidegger, Gadamer also emphasized the continuing narrative and baggage of our own lives and the evolving 'life' of the work. Since we are from a different place and time from the author, we can only understand when the two narratives (work and viewer) happily meet; which he called the 'fusion of horizons.' (Gadamer was content with this predicament and believed this must take place for any genuine understanding.)

However, Intentist maintain that this is a narrative argument and was formed and developed as a discursive model applied to writing. It is therefore very effective when interpreting texts since they clearly are narratorial and linear. We generally start and finish at the same place, reading letters and words sequentially. We discover the 'world of' and 'in front of' the text (a theory developed by Paul Ricoeur) incrementally in space and time as both the texts and we develop. However, Gadamer, Barthes, Foucault and Derrida have all used this established literary theory to understand fine art. Intentism as an arts movement argues that this theory overreaches itself. The reason is that many arts such as painting, sculpture and photography are **anarrative.** There is no 'order of experience expectation' in these art forms. This is to say that although artists might consciously or unconsciously construct certain shapes that by size or colour capture the viewer's attention first, the very precise order or letters, words, sentences, paragraphs etc that a work is made from is far more inflexible. Furthermore, there are no public rules that say an artist can't ignore perspective or colour theory in his work that parallel the public rules of language or genre. Of course, in poetry there is far more room to play with language conventions, but only a certain degree before the work moves from language to conceptual art. Without these public rules we can either echo French philosopher Jacques Derrida that 'meaning is constantly deferred' or we need to know authorial intentions.

Secondly, French Algerian-born philosopher Jacques Derrida, 1930-2004, amongst many things coined the terms 'deconstruction' and 'undecideables.' Deconstruction has become common parlance, but even in his lifetime Derrida decried the fact that it had been misunderstood. In itself this is ironic in that to use it correctly, one would assume that the speaker should adopt the author's (Derrida) intended meaning for it. Derrida wrote that the text should be turned in on itself to be deconstructed. Very often this had the effect of discovering contradictory meanings in the same text. He also spoke of undecideables and 'la difference' and 'play.' His writing is highly complex but in essence he maintained that the meaning of any work is always deferred in that you can never get a final meaning of anything and consequently that a single line of text or an artwork must always have more than one meaning. Intentists would like to ask whether this includes his own writing?

Jacques Derrida

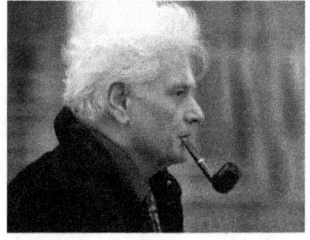

There is always more than one meaning.

Thirdly, French philosopher Roland Barthes wrote a seminal work in 1967 entitled 'The Death of the Author' whereby he concluded that as any work is just 'a textile of quotations' nothing is wholly original and therefore nothing has a creator or author; the author or artist has died. It is surely indisputable that every creator is influenced by his schemata. But does that mean that there is no such thing as singularity of authorship? Any artist will consciously or unconsciously select from innumerable sources as we don't create 'ex nihilo.' However, this collection or reordering can be unique. Similarly, most of the sentences in this book although using common words have never been said in this order before.

Roland Barthes

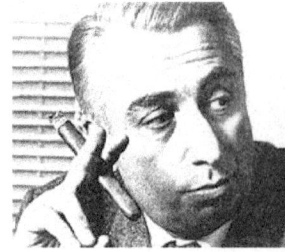

French Philosopher coined the term 'the death of the author.'

Lastly, French philosopher Michel Foucault was deeply influential in this debate. Foucault lived from 1926-1984 and penned a work influenced by his friend Barthes entitled, 'Qu'est-ce qu'un auteur?' (What is an Author?) in 1969. One of his central arguments is that authorship is only a recent construct since the advent of copyright as authors wanted to protect their rights.

All these leading figures argued that everything we do is the consequence of the personal baggage of where we have come from. Therefore, we can apply this argument to the philosophers themselves. What were the socio-political influences during the period these thinkers were active? Can we trace the rejection of authorship and with it intention back to a wider context?

Michel Foucault

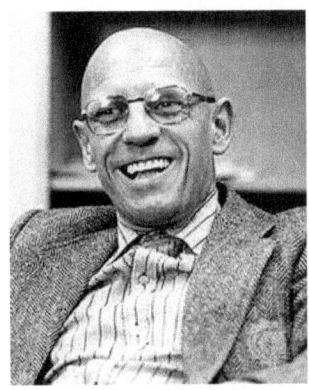

Continental philosopher Michel Foucault

ii)   The Rise and Fall of Modernism.

Modernism had its roots in the Renaissance and the Enlightenment. It was chiefly Humanist and optimistic. With Reason and knowledge, Mankind could get to the Truth and with truth mankind had a bright future.

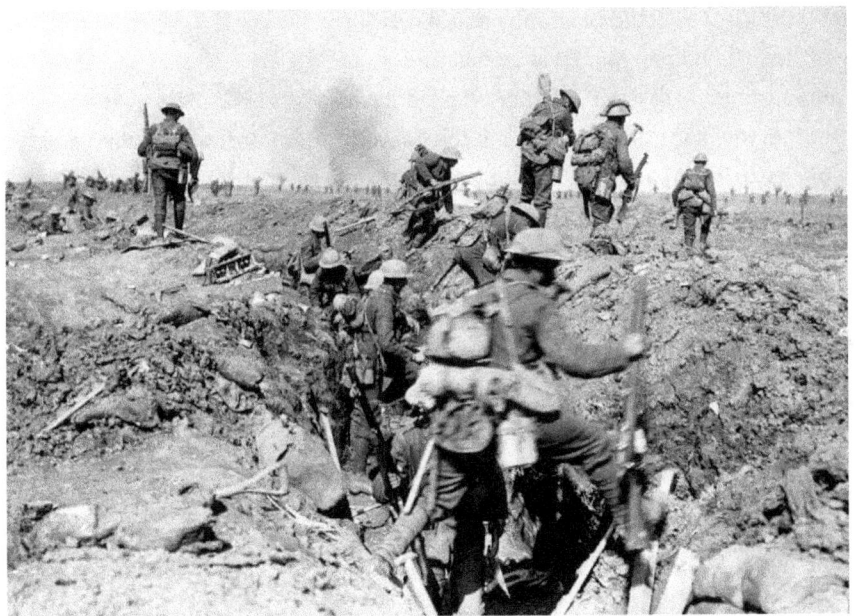

FIGURE 1 THE BATTLE OF THE SOMME 1916

Professor of philosophy and author of 'Aesthetics' Colin Lyas believes the Battle of the Somme in 1916 was a 'turning point' in the humanist optimism that had pervaded thinking for several centuries.

On its first day there were 60,000 British casualties and over 1.5 million casualties by the end of the Battle. This had such a dehumanizing effect and according to Lyas, the Humanistic optimism of Modernism never recovered. Lyas suggests that this suddenly rendered the soldiers and by extension people as numbers and this nihilistic attitude began to derail the importance of the human author in works.

New Criticism (approx. 1920's - 1960's)

Within a couple of years of the end of WW1 a new theory for literature emerged called New Criticism. New Criticism rejected biography and sociological matters. The human mind was considered unimportant. In essence, the period a work was created, the place, the creator, and the author's intentions (often called a work's **extrinsics**) all had absolutely no influence on what the work meant and could mean in the future.

The Intentional Fallacy (1946)

The Death blow to Modernism and optimism was The Second World War. National Socialism came from one of the most educated, advanced nations on earth. One year on Wimsatt and Beardsely wrote the Intentional Fallacy. In this document the writers argued that firstly, intention was impossible to find. Secondly, that even if the intention of the artist was known perfectly, this had no effect on interpreting a work.

The 1968 Paris Student Riots

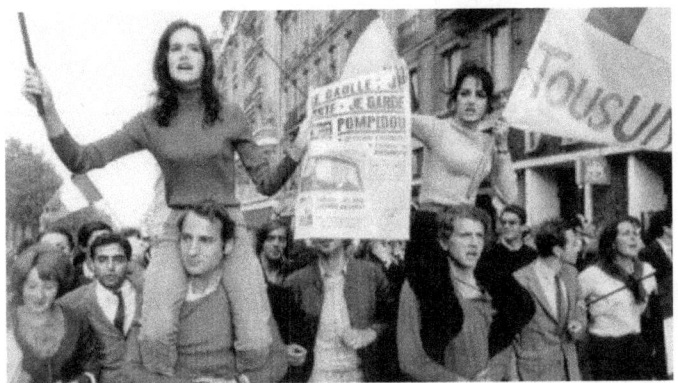

FIGURE 2 STUDENTS AND WORKERS IN PARIS

The 1968 student riots were the largest ever general strike of an industrialized country. Students were joined by up to ten million workers

Such was the upheaval to the establishment that they nearly caused the collapse of the government. The events permanently broke traditional views of education, gender, politics, and many other world views. It was during this period of instability that Roland Barthes wrote of the 'death of the author.' The Author was seen as an illegitimate 'authority' that controlled the meaning of a work, and like the governmental authorities, must be stopped.

PART TWO - WHERE CAN MEANING BE FOUND?

1. The Work

i) Literature

Let's begin with literature as the theorists we have introduced so far all worked mainly in literature. The father of modern linguistics, Ferdinand de Saussure taught that language is composed of arbitrary sounds. There is nothing 'cow-like' about a cow. This is clearly demonstrated by the fact that other languages have very different words for this animal. Another simple example of this is the meaning of the word 'nada.' In Spanish it means 'nothing', in Hindi it refers to 'thread' and in Indonesian it signifies 'tone.' If 'nada' was not an arbitrary sound, then all languages would have a variance on the word for that concept.

We understand words because they are **different** from other words. More recent linguistics has shown that there are a few exceptions to this. Onomatopoeia is the formation of a word from a sound associated with what is named. The Harvard psychologist and author Stephen Pinker has also written extensively about how some sounds in English are predominantly linked to constructs such as size. However, for the majority of lexis, Saussure's understanding still holds true. This immediately causes difficulties in interpretation. If words are arbitrary sounds, where does meaning come from? Literary theorist Stanley Fish may say meaning comes from 'interpretative communities', but Intentists would argue that so does the author's intention.

"The connection between the signifier and the signified is arbitrary."

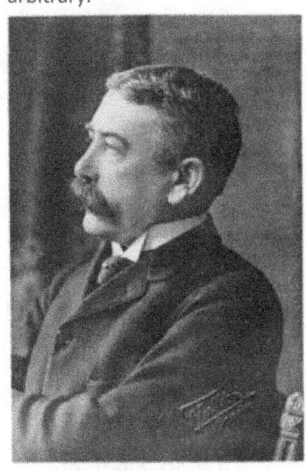

Ferdinand de Saussure

Another interpretative difficulty comes down to what language is for. Linguist Noam Chomsky believes that language is essentially for the mind as a tool to understand the world and only secondarily for communication. If this is true, then surely the mind that creates the internal texts has a say in its meaning. Moreover, if this is true, the belief that the reader or viewer's meaning often trumps the author (Derrida, Barthes, Foucault) is harder to argue since 99 per cent of all linguistic texts are only internal.

Contrary to this theory espoused by Chomsky is the much more commonly held opinion that language is essentially a tool for communication. Austrian-British philosopher Ludwig Wittgenstein famously said that language is essentially public. We share a common lexis. However, there are also interpretative difficulties here. Language is in a permanently vulnerable to flux. A brief listen to your teenage relative will inform you that every nut and bolt of language (noun, verb, adjective and adverb) is not immune to change in use. There is not one part of speech that is free from it. Moreover, it is almost impossible to predict when or what word might be affected.

For example, various verbs, nouns, adjectives and question tags have and will continue to liable to change in function and usage. If all four of these areas of language can change, then perhaps any of the grammatical nuts and bolts of language can change. Modern linguists have made predictions in relation to English. Since English is, at present, the lingua-franca of the world, certain problem areas for speakers with a different mother tongue may disappear. These include the third person 's', the 'th' sound and the present perfect.

Let's have a look at some of the examples noted above:

1.Stative and dynamic verbs. E.g. 'I'm lovin' it.'

Stative verbs describe states; for example, the verb 'to be.' On the other hand, dynamic verbs describe situation where something is happening.
Consequently, 'I *aming* Vittorio' would be ungrammatical and non-sensical. Conversely, a dynamic verb, such as 'to walk' can be used both as a gerund (an 'ing' verb functioning like a noun) 'walking is good for you,' and as a present participle,' I am walking.' Love, on the other hand, is a stative verb, and hence

'loving' has been considered incorrect. However, the infamous MacDonald's slogan is *'I'm lovin' it'*. Consequently, 'I'm loving', 'I'm hating' and many others are becoming common place. Grammar books published in the last the last ten years are making this point.

2. Nouns. E.g. 'WAG.'

'Wag', has been understood as a verb (for example, to wag your finger) for many years, however, in recent years it has become an acronym for Wives And Girlfriends of famous footballers.

3. Adjectives. E.g 'Gay.'

The adjective 'gay' has meant 'happy' for generations and now is generally used to mean homosexual. In fact, its usage today to refer to being happy has all but died.

4. Tag questions. E.g. 'He likes you, in it?'

Tag questions are question forms placed at the end of statements to converts them into questions. There are specific rules for them. Firstly, the verb in the question form must correspond to the verb in the statement. For example, 'That can't be him, can it?' is correct because in both clauses the verb 'can' is used. Secondly, if the statement is negative, the tag must be positive and vice versa. Examples would include ' He did this, didn't he?' and 'He didn't go there, did he?' However, in the example above, which is a widely used template today, there are two grammatical inconsistencies. First, an incorrect verb is used in the tag question; it should be the auxiliary 'does' not 'is', and secondly its form needs to be negative as the statement is positive. In sum the 'correct' sentence should read as follows: He likes you, doesn't he?

Arguably, there could be no sacred area of language that could not begin to leave its traditional epistemological moorings at any time. Finally, it would be not inappropriate to conclude that language is constantly vulnerable to flux in grammar and meaning. This is not in question for both postmodern literary theorists and Intentists. The difference is that Intentists believe that all the major epistemological qualities are fixed when the writer puts down his pen and it behoves any reader with concern for exegesis to look at the original intended meaning of a piece of lexis.

Therefore, is meaning found in the work? The New Critics argued that any epistemological qualities can only be intrinsic (in the work alone). However, looking at texts it is far from certain that the work alone can always give us a fixed meaning. Later in this book we will look at the other two main sources for meaning: the reader/viewer/interpretative community and the author.

You may have noticed that we have just alluded to 'a fixed meaning.' Of course, a fixed meaning may not always be what you desire and Intentists have sometimes been the subject of criticism on this point. However, Intentists maintain that their position actually frees up the work for wider interpretation. There argument comes from an extension of J.L. Austin's Speech Acts. This theory has later been adopted and refined by John Searle and Vanhoozer but essentially divides language into three Speech Acts: locutionary, illocutionary and perlocutionary. Locutionary speech acts are the utterances themselves with all syntactic and semantic aspects. Illoctionary acts include the intended significance of the work as a socially valid verbal action. Finally, perlocutionary acts include its actual effect whether intended or not. Intentists have also reinterpreted Speech Acts through the lens of intention to argue that intention alone gives a work most freedom. For example, if the artist intends a work to be as open to interpretation as possible, then he or she will stop at the locutionary stage. The text or work will have properties that categorize it as a work. However, there is no attempt to persuade the reader or viewer into any interpretation. Conversely, if a creator intends the work to have a specific meaning – for example, a document of rules and regulations then his or her work will have an illocutionary force with intended functions to warn or inform. Moreover, the writer will directly or indirectly encourage the reader to understand the text in this manner – the perlocutionary force. Intentists argue that this position is liberating. For example, a New Critic who believes that meaning is found in the work alone would supposedly accept the theory of locutionary acts but the work can never be a text with a singular message. Moreover, post-structuralists may be very happy to argue for perlocutionary acts, but what if a creator wanted to put a specific message across? In conclusion, Intentists believe an author makes a work and chooses whether that work has insignificant to very specific meaningful intention and so a work can be anything from highly ambiguous to direct and singularly meaningful.

ii)   The Visual Arts

If language is essentially arbitrary and constantly changing, are the visual arts any different? Certainly, the visual arts often have clear representations of the physical world, and yet, a work's meaning can remain to a lesser or greater extent, ambiguous.

For the sake of this study, the visuals arts will be distilled down into two areas: firstly, colour, and secondly, shape and gesture.

1. Colour

Are colours ambiguous? There are several associations of red that seem to be common across cultures. These include speed, passion, love, blood and fire. However, even here it is impossible to distinguish universal nature and nurture in that to untangle which connections are hard-wired in our brains and which have highly common associations in our first years of life is highly complex.

Nevertheless, these significances are often used in marketing strategies. For example, fast food outlets. However, red has the following culturally dependent associations:

China- celebration and luck

India – Purity

Russia – beauty

South Africa – mourning.

Consequently, an abstract image in red may be interpreted very differently in South Africa and China.

Secondly, blue certainly has apparent universal associations that include calmness, sea and water. Again, however, there are several other culturally dependent connections:

China - immortality

Israel – holiness

US and Europe – sadness

Iran – mourning

Therefore, an image may be associated as being melancholy in the US and Europe, yet holy in Israel.

Green universally may relate to nature, the environment, money and envy, yet, once more, there are many more variable associations:

China – green hats may mean a wife is cheating

India – Islam

Ireland – religious and patriotic significance

Some tropical countries – danger

Hence, a green image may be linked with Islam in India and Roman Catholicism in Ireland.

White, has international associations with purity, winter and spirituality, yet can be associated with the following:

Eastern Cultures – death

The US and Europe – purity

China – age, autumn, misfortune

Consequently, white representing purity in the US and Europe, may be associated with death in Eastern cultures.

2. Shapes

Since shapes have structure and detail that colour does not, it may be assumed that they are less likely to have multiple associations. However, this is frequently not the case.

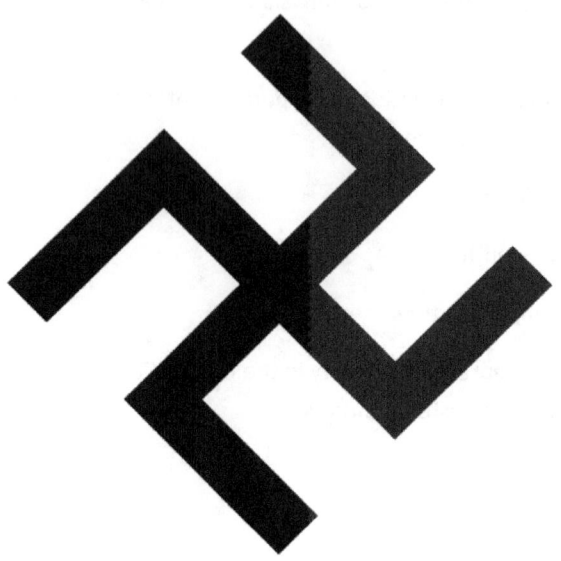

For the majority of people, the first association with this symbol would most probably be National Socialism.

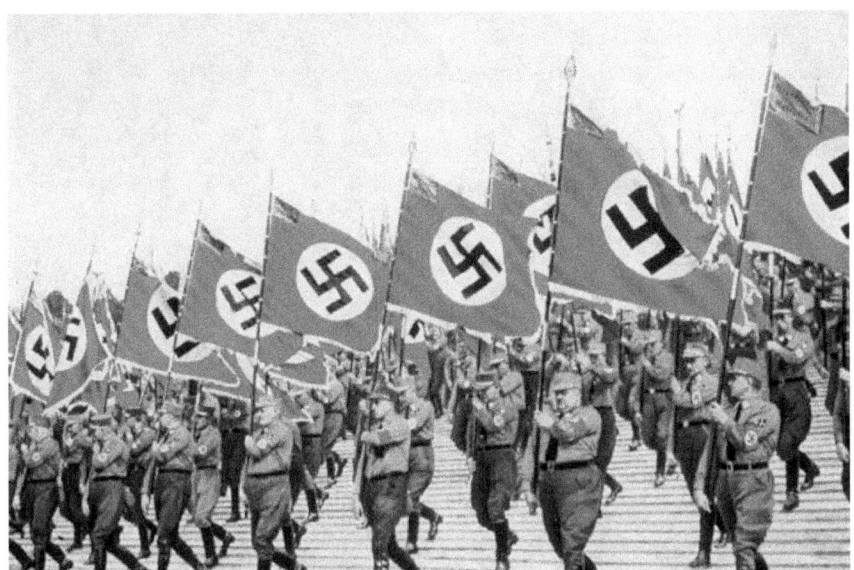

FIGURE 4 NATIONAL SOCIALISTS DURING WW2

Since this is the primary association, would it be correct to assume the image symbolizes Nazism if found in a work of art? Certainly, if meaning is found in the work alone and as the New Critics maintained, if meaning can change over time, presumably any work that has this symbol before the advent of Nazism must signify National Socialism today.

In fact, this symbol has been mirrored on the chest of the Buddha and yet it still carries the same basic design.

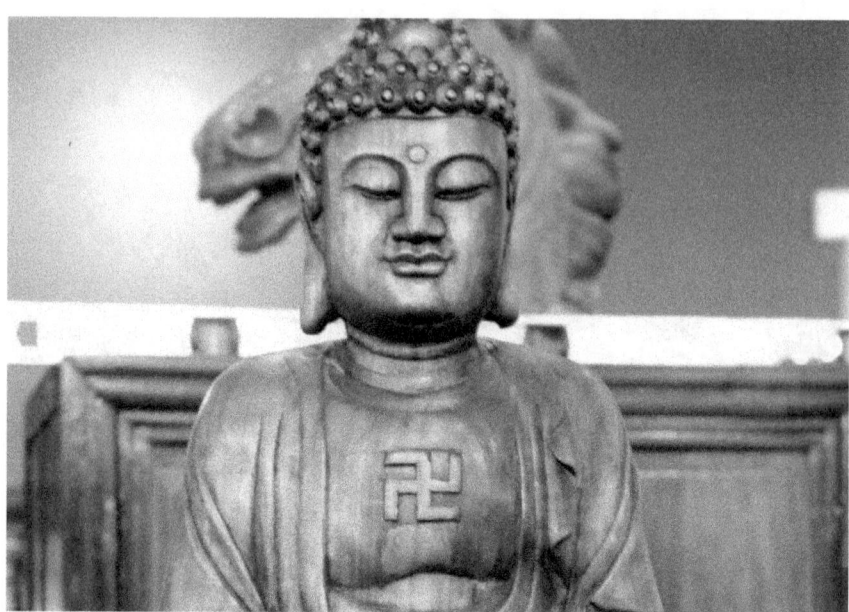

The symbol represents Nirvana; the state of being free from suffering. Consequently, a work of art displaying this symbol might represent all that is associated with National Socialism or freedom from suffering – Nirvana. It may be fine to play with these concepts in a creative essay, but any serious historian will want to know what the meaning of this symbol was to its creator and the people of the day.

The same symbol can be found in many other places, with a wide variety of associations. Some of these significances are the following:

- A sacred symbol in Hinduism, Buddhism, Jainism and Shamanism
- Found on many Buddhist and Hindu temples
- Found on ancient Greek coins, clothing and architecture
- Ancient Armenians used it to symbolize the sun
- Used in Baltic art to symbolize the 'god of thunder.'
- A decoration for Easter eggs in Slavic culture during the renaissance
- In certain churches
- In Freemasonry

The icon of the cross has similarly multiple associations.

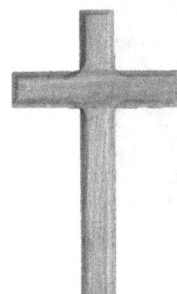

Western culture naturally associates the cross with Christianity and the crucifixion of Jesus Christ. However, there are other associates that both pe-date and come after Christianity. A historian might link the symbol not to one death in particular, but to the most brutal form of Roman capital punishment. However, a similar symbol is the Egyptian Ankh and recently as part of a necklace, it has become a symbol of fashion and sexuality.

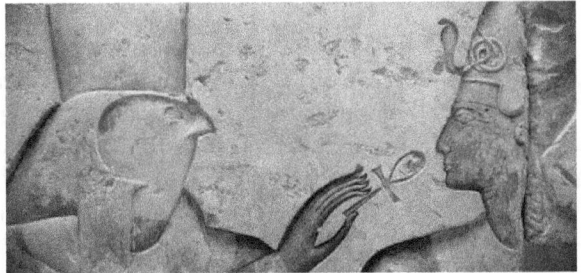

FIGURE 6 THE EGYPTIAN ANKH IS OFTEN CALLED 'THE KEY OF LIFE.'

3. Gestures

Another important element of art, particularly in figurative work, is the gesture; think of the raised index finger in Leonardo da Vinci's *The Last Supper* and *St. John the Baptist*. Is it possible to know from the work alone and without extrinsic knowledge of biography or time and culture what a gesture means?

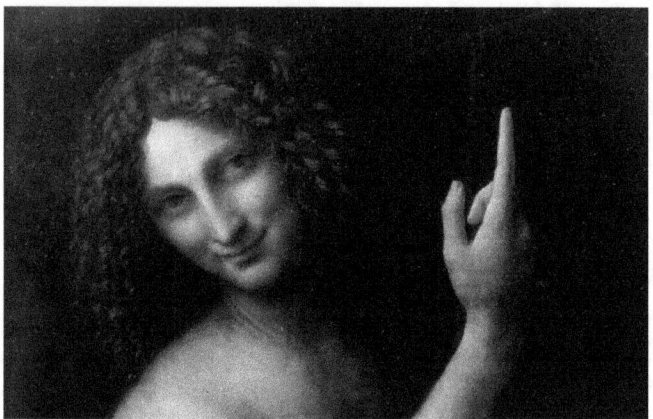

FIGURE 7 DA VINCI'S JOHN THE BAPTIST

This gesture below signifies 'OK' in many countries.

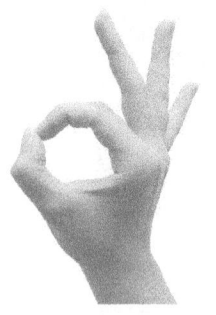

However, in Brazil and Germany it can also refer to anal sex and is considered rude and offensive. In Japan, it signifies money and in France it represents 'zero' or 'worthless.'

This is just one of many other gestures involving the hands, head and feet that can be culturally dependent for meaning.

iii) Case Studies

Child Art

Let us put Intentism's original arguments against New Criticism in the form of a case study. Remember the original question? Is meaning found solely in the work?

We have seen that for texts and visual art most properties can have multiple associations. Therefore, the following case study will look squarely at something espoused by much postmodern criticism, namely that these associations can all be equally true and valid meanings of a work. In essence, the work can mean whatever each viewer or interpretative community wants it to mean; epistemological pluralism. It most be noted that French philosopher Jacques Derrida has written that work does not have an infinite number of meanings, but more than one. Intentists would argue that Derrida never gives clear criteria or guidelines to explain when an interpretation is valid and when it is not.

Imagine a young child who one day decides to draw a picture of his or her mother. Due to the child's age, the work bears little resemblance to her. However, the child proudly displays the work to his or her father and declares that he or she has drawn mummy. If the meaning is solely in the work, the father would have no choice but to disagree with the child. Perhaps the father would say it represents instead a monster, since it resembles a monster more than a mother.

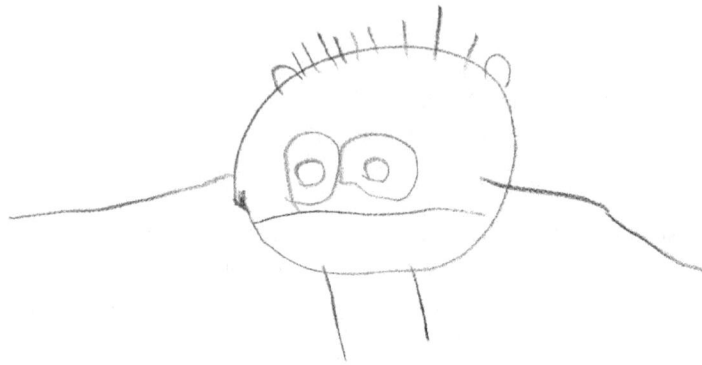

FIGURE 8 A YOUNG CHILD'S PENCIL DRAWING

Is this the correct response? After all the work does resemble a monster more than a mother.

No, the picture is of the mother. Contrary to New Criticism, the work is not the sole desirable place to find meaning. Contrary to much of postmodern criticism, the work does not have a different meaning for the son and the father. The reason for this is that the work is not the meaning, the work is the vehicle for the meaning. In this case, the work means 'mother' and most probably the child will grow up and improve the quality of his 'vehicles' so they resemble more accurately his or her intentions.

There are two other points that need to be made here. Firstly, this case study is not trying to understand all the psychological baggage of the child. There may well be various reasons (apart from a lack of skill) for the child to have drawn his or her mother this way. These are separated by most Intentists as the various 'causes' of the work rather than the intention. Secondly, other Intentists may argue for a weaker or partial intentionalism in this example. Their position would be that intentions include conscious and conscious performance expectations and that for the work to mean what it was intended to mean, requires the intention to be 'realized' in the work. The result of this is that some Intentists would maintain that the child has not realized his or her intentions and therefore the work cannot be unambiguously defined as the artist's mother. A difficulty that arises from this position is that the interpretation of the viewer has trumped the intention of the creator. If this is the case, then does the ultimate authority in matters of meaning rest with the viewer once more?

Two further areas illustrate the shortcomings of New Criticism's confidence that meaning can be found in the work alone: irony and ambiguities.

Irony

Without reference to the human mind, irony and sarcasm cannot always be understood. Indeed, it is ironic that Wimsatt and Beardsley authors of the Intentional fallacy (1946) has used irony to argue their New Critics position. They stated that the only means of understanding irony is to compare the work with the viewer's understanding of what the work would normally mean. If there is incongruity, then the work may be ironic. However, the tension between work and reader may not be as apparent at the time of reading. The only sure indication is to compare the works ostensive meaning with the creator's intent.

A work such as Big Breakfast would be unintelligible and self contradictory unless linked to the human creative intender.

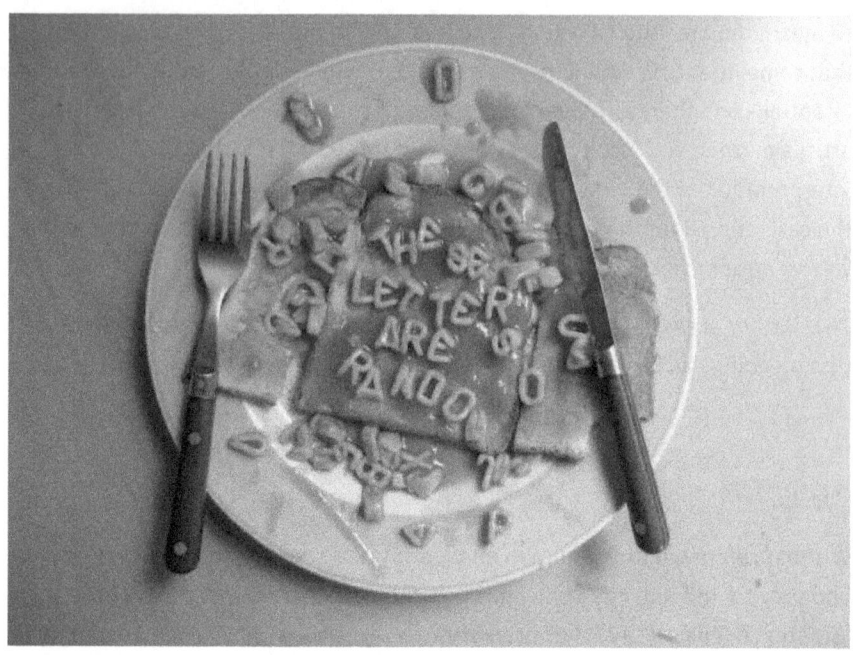

Figure 9 Luciano Pelosi's big breakfast

To a New Critic there would appear to be two ways to read this work. Firstly, the New Critic would look at the work, believe that all meaning is found in the work alone, agree with Wittengstein that there is some sort of shared vocabulary and read 'These letters are random.' If the meaning is in the text alone and these letters are random, then of course the sentence would have no meaning but the decision to conclude that the work is random would to some measure be from out of the work. The New Critic would be forced to deny that meaning is found in the text alone as it is clearly self contradictory.

The four images, linked in the form of a photobooth series, feature the sitter with a silver necklace. On the sitter's necklace hang words. Each succeeding image features the next word in the sentence' These are not Linked.'

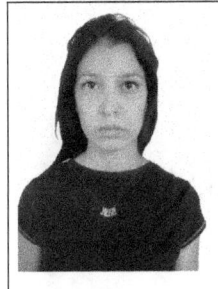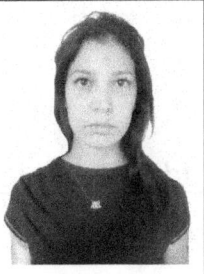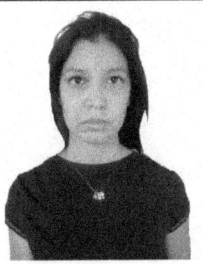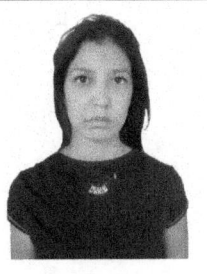

Quite clearly, not only are the words linked on the chain, but they are linked grammatically and semantically. The same problems associated with the New Critics' reading of 'Big Breakfast' can apply to this work.

Textual Ambiguities

This is another area where meaning is clearly not found in the work alone. The reader needs to accept the ambiguity, ask the writer for clarification or hope that by reading on the meaning may become clearer.

Here is a TV listings with particularly unclear descriptions.

5.oo Secret Millionaire. Reality show. The millionaire gets physically attacked for lateness at work Unfortunate Jon Davies is the richest participant, well at least he's a millionaire.
6.00 The Sunday Kitchen. Chef Gordon Ramsay demonstrates at a Summer School in Mumbai the best way to prepare hot food and create drinks that are cool.
7.00 Panorama. Report into why it can take many elderly people with a common cold several weeks to be better.
8.00 The School Run. Reality Show. Teacher James Howells speaks to several students whose work remains outstanding. Including conversations with students as to why some actually enjoy annoying teachers.
10.00 Simon Cowell Uncut: Pier's Morgan's Life Stories. Interview where Simon Cowell discusses his life and career with Piers Morgan.
11.00 News Shorts. Do the police need greater restrictions ass CCTV shows police hitting man with cane.

iv) <u>Final Thoughts</u>

<u>Works need to have an 'intender' to have a meaning</u>

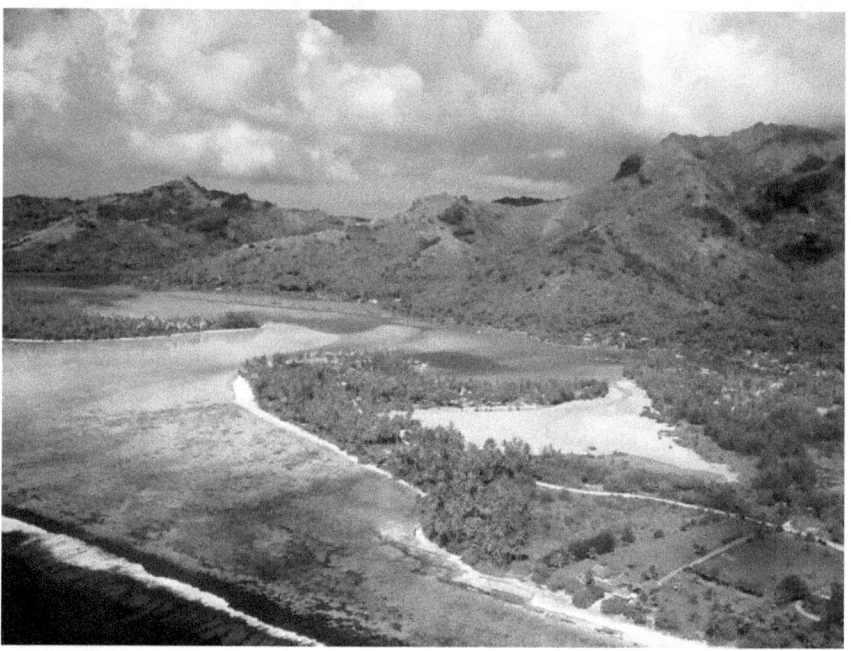

The question 'What is the above picture of?' appears to be straight forward; nature. However, what does nature 'mean'? The answer is more ambiguous. If the question is addressed to a believer in a divine Creator, then nature would be assumed to be the creative order of God. Therefore, there would be an intender, and the world, as God's creation, does have meaning, which is often understood to be to reveal God' glory.

Conversely, if the question is addressed to a person who does not believe in a creator, then the answer would surely be that nature has no meaning. The reason being because there is no intender and consequently, nature has no aim or purpose. It is significant that when evolutionary biologist and Atheist

Richard Dawkins is asked a 'why' question about the universe, he becomes understandably, critical. He is aware that science without God can only answer 'how' questions.

Intentist would argue this is an important distinction. If we assume the universe was not intentionally created, then we quite rightly dismiss claims for it to have meaning. However, many critics try and marry a belief that the author's intention has no relevance to a work and that there is meaning to be discovered.

Parrot speech

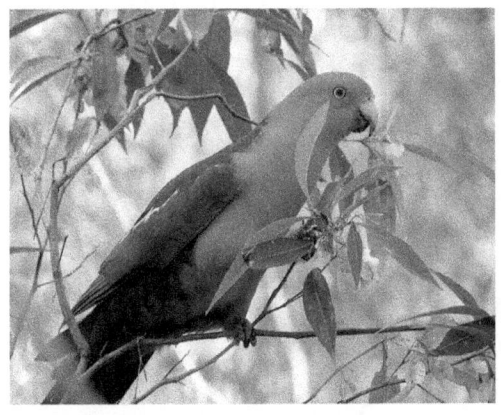

Another example would be a parrot that has been taught to utter certain words. If the parrot is heard to utter racist or other offensive words, should the parrot be held accountable? To the parrot there is no difference between offensive language and words of kindness: they are arbitrary sounds. In sum the difference between the words of a parrot and the words of a human is that in the second the arbitrary sounds are imbued with meaning by the mind of the intender.

Works speak of the human mind behind it

When critics or readers discuss a work of art it is very common to use adjectives of the mind, for example, sensitive, naive, intelligent etc. Many philosophers including Prof. Colin Lyas have argued that we instinctively attribute human mental qualities to a work since we know that the work is an expression of a creative mind.

2 The Viewer and the Interpretative Community

In the previous section, the question addressed was whether meaning is found in the work. The answer given was 'not entirely'. This section will consider whether meaning is found in the viewer/reader's response. The answer, according to Intentists, is in the negative.

If meaning were to be found with the viewer there would be two consequences. Firstly, an art historian and an uneducated child with opposing interpretations would both be equally correct. This would put into question the entire educational system. What would be the merit in studying? What would be the reason behind lecturer's salaries if there is no hierarchy of interpretations?

The second consequence of meaning being found in the viewer/reader's response would be that there might be as many meanings as viewers. Derrida, as we mentioned earlier in fact did not subscribe to this position and wrote that there are some things a work cannot mean. However, once deconstruction is exercised and 'undecideables' are sought, once the creator's intention is considered undesirable and once the Birth of the Viewer is celebrated, Derrida and many postmodernists completely fail to implement any alternative framework that can exclude wayward interpretations.

Consequently, two conclusions could be asserted:

Firstly, all learning is worthless. No opinion is better informed. The work that was considered racist at the beginning of this book would still mean that to that viewer. Therefore, whatever the artist's intentions are, the work at least to one person is racist. Intentists would make the distinction here between offensive and racist. A work could have the best intentions and still be offensive as the focus here is on the viewer's emotional response. However, a racist work focuses more on the work (and with that the intentions) than the response. Intentists have argued that it is much easier to believe that work has a life of its own when their own work is not judged. Historical examples of this include Derrida's response to a critique by John Searle. Derrida responded in a rebuttal of over ninety pages arguing that Searle misunderstood his position and it should have been clear. Intentists have stressed that this is hypocrisy.

Another controversial argument relates to German philosopher Martin Heidegger. It came to light that Heidegger not only supported National Socialism but had written several papers praising Hitler and his party. It has been interesting to notice how many critics who believe that the author is separate from the work have looked at Heidegger's body of work differently.

Secondly, if the work can mean anything, in a sense it means nothing. Furthermore, a logical possibility could be that a creator may decide that the work means anything and a viewer may conclude that the work means nothing. Implausibly, both mutually exclusive meanings would be equally valid and true.

i)   Meaning and Significance

Intentist would admit that viewers can interpret works differently. Furthermore, there is little doubt that culture, personality and generational differences can influence interpretations. This is undeniable. Moreover, many art critics would stress that this very fact enriches art as it affects and moves people differently.

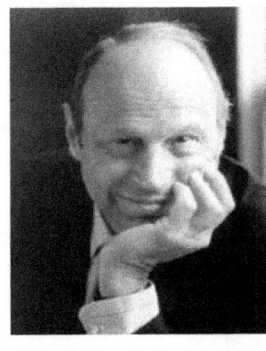

Figure 10 E.D. Hirsch

The literary critic E.D.Hirsch Jnr understood these changes in interpretations by epistemologically dividing 'meaning' and 'significance.' As mentioned previously, Gadamer had proposed the 'effective history of the work.' This term explained how a work has a history, or life and at different times and in different places, the work's meaning changes. In effect, the work can never settle with a fixed meaning.

Intentism, conversely, agrees with Hirsch that the last intention an intender makes, *is to intend no more,* and at this moment all the epistemological qualities of the work are present, and consequently, the meaning is fixed. Therefore, what changes in time and place is not the meaning of the work, but people's associations of it, or as Hirsch has written, the **significances** of it.

It is part of the power and unique influence of the arts that people can take different things from a work. This is to be celebrated. Yet according to the Intentists these significances should never be confused with meanings.

> *It must be noted at this point that Hirsch was primarily referring to texts and many Intentists consider the inference of 'significance' to be too weak for the impact different interpretations can have on a viewer.*

Perhaps the difference between meaning and significance can be understood more clearly through two case studies.

Case Studies

1. A Statue in Piccadilly Circus, London

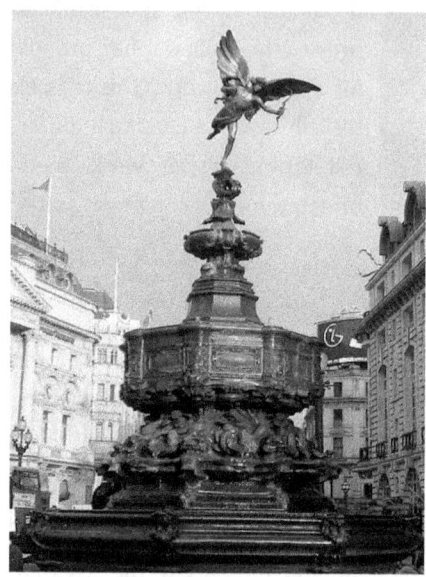

Eros or Anteros?

The statue above in Piccadilly Circus, London must be one of the most well-known landmarks in London. It was built in 1885, but what does the sculpture depict? It is popularly known as Eros. Some people believe it to be The Angel of Christian Charity. Yet what was the original commission? Artist Alfred Gilbert intended the figure to be Anteros, the Greek god of requited love. The sculpture was intended to symbolize the selfless philanthropic love of the Earl of Shaftesbury for the poor and this is what it means today. This case study illustrates that even if the majority assumes a position contrary to the artist's intention, this position is still a significance or association; the meaning does not change.

2. Che Guevara

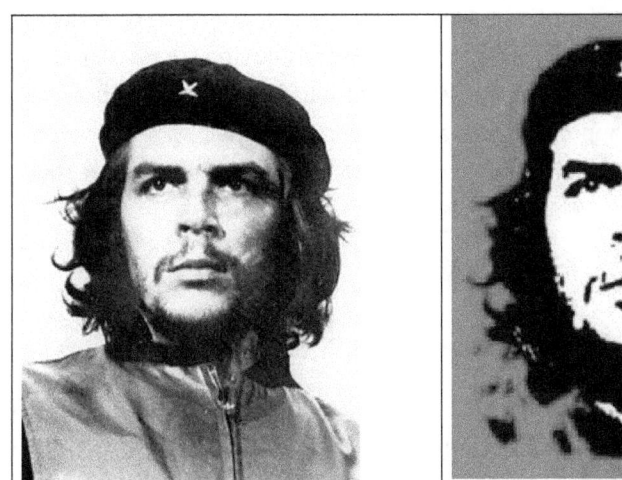

In 1960 the photographer Alberto Korda took a photo of Marxist revolutionary Che Guevara. Korda had an original intention for the artwork and realised it in the photograph. The Photograph of Che Guevara was taken on March 5, 1960 by Alberto Korda at a funeral service for victims of the La Coubre explosion.

Since then, the photo has reached iconographic status and has come to represent many different things such as 'revolution', 'justice' and even 'coolness' amongst teenage students. Are these associations new meanings of the original photograph unintended by the original artist?

In the case of the Che Guevara image two different processes have taken place. Firstly, people can appropriate an artwork and thereby give the artwork a new 'significance' (not a new meaning). As discussed earlier, the distinction between 'significance' and 'meaning' is an important one. The person who creates the artwork is responsible for the meaning, not the one who 'receives' it. Yet the receiver can choose to attribute a certain significance to the artwork. This significance can be personal, one of many 'significances' and can even be in conflict with the meaning but should never be termed a 'new meaning'. In this way individuals and communities chose to give Korda's photograph a new significance.

Secondly, the original photograph was adapted by Jim Fitzpatrick in 1967 in order to create the heavily stylised posters with the red background that often featured on teenage students' bedroom walls in the 1970s. Fitzpatrick took the artwork and used it to realise a new artistic intention, thereby creating a new artwork based upon a previous artwork. Intentism argues 'no creative input, no meaning input.' An accusation against Intentism has been how to gauge when a work has been appropriated in a new context, adding new significances and when the appropriation is creative enough to make a new work and a new meaning.

3. 'Our Song'

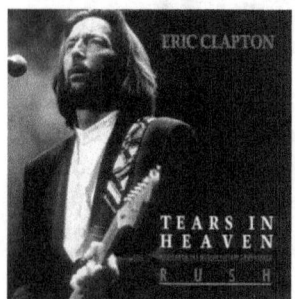

The second case study looks at the exceptional ownership listeners have towards music. An example of this would be lovers who might refer to a piece of music as 'our song.'

'Tears in Heaven' is a ballad written by Eric Clapton and Will Jennings about the pain felt following the death of his four-year-old son, Conor, who fell from a window of the 53rd- floor New York apartment of his mother's friend, on March 20th, 1991. However, it has been voted as one of the top tearjerker songs and has become associated not only with the death of loved ones, but periods of sadness in other areas. These responses are considered by Intentists as significances, not new meanings. To Intentists, the weakness of 'significance' in its connotations is most apparent in the power of music.

However, Intentists would also maintain that Eric Clapton's song emphasizes the power of the human input in creation. Far from the removal of the author, knowing the deeply moving biographical background to the work only adds to its impact.

4.Le Bateau by Henri Matisse

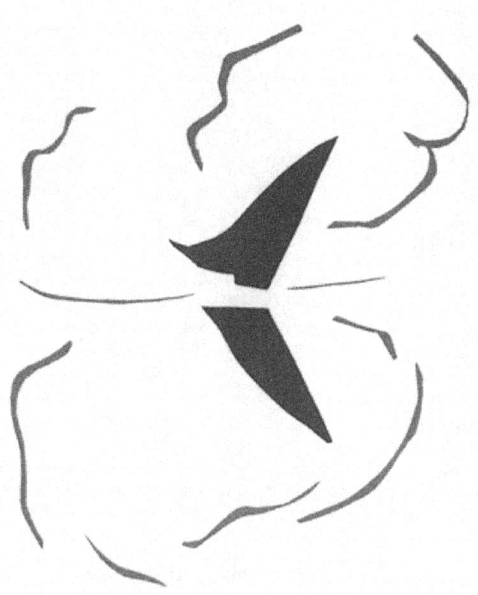

Le Bateau caused a minor stir when The Museum of Modern Art, in New York, which housed it, hung the print upside-down for forty-six days in 1961 until Genevieve Habert, a stockbroker, noticed the mistake and notified a guard. Subsequently, Habert informed the New York Times who in turn notified Monroe Wheeler, the museum's art director. As a result, the artwork was rehung. However, if meaning is found with the viewer, and the majority of the gallery's visitors believed it to be the correct way up, if the curators (who were of course, also viewers) took the print to be originally the right way up, then surely that constitutes a valid meaning and the work should have been left this way. Since, there is no hierarchy of interpretation, since the intention of the artist is not of value, why was it rehung? What theory or principle was the rehanging being conformed to? Undoubtably the work was changed to reflect the artist's intention, biography and other extrinsics.

5.Two cockerels by Pablo Picasso

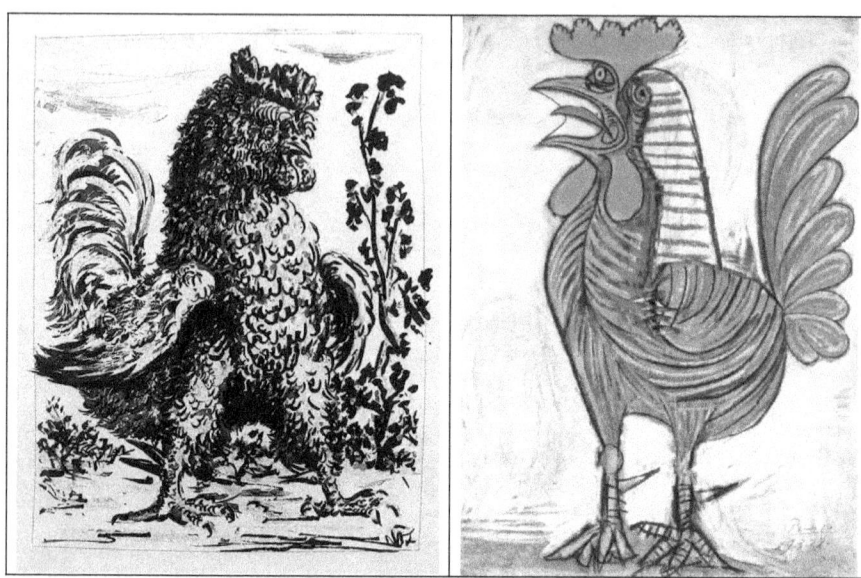

The first of these is a beautiful illustration for Buffon's Natural History, the second is a caricature. Art historian E.H. Gombrich in his seminal 'The Story of Art' makes the point that, given the first of these pictures, no one could deny Picasso's ability to make lifelike representations. Knowing this, when the second drawing is observed and noted that it bears less resemblance to a cockerel, it would be foolish to dismiss it. Instead, other questions should be considered, such as what was Picasso intending? In other words, being aware of Picasso's oeuvre can help provide understanding as to the creator's intentions in a work. If a viewer assumes that Picasso was an incompetent draughtsman by solely looking at the first image it would be a wrong interpretation.

In summary, this chapter has looked at whether meaning is found from the viewer and according to Intentists, meaning does not reside in the viewer's interpretation alone.

3. The Artist's Intention

i) Difficulties for the artist to access their intentions

Intentists maintain that meaning is found in the creator's intention. Intentists make up a wide variety of intentionalists from partial intentionalists to stronger forms. Partial intentionalists believe that interpretation must include where possible, the author's intentions. However, they would define intention as a 'performance expectation' and therefore it may not be successfully realized in the work. When it isn't, it would be inaccurate to force the intention onto the viewer. Stronger forms of intentionalists would argue that the final say is always with the artist's intention. Conversely, the New Critics have argued that even if it were possible to discover the writer or artist's intention, it would not be useful for interpretation. The doubt in Wimsatt and Beardsley mind as to whether an intention can ever be objectively discovered will be looked at in this section.

One of the greatest influences on both New Criticism and Postmodernism was psychology. One of its leading figures was Sigmund Freud, author of the seminal work 'Dreams' published in 1900. The human mind was understood to be profoundly complex, and the psychological baggage that we bring to everything was put at the forefront of analysis. The unconscious, in particular, was considered a profound influence. It was consequently only natural that questions would arise regarding intentionalism. Is the creator ever fully aware of his intentions? Can he or she ever fully know the meaning of his or her work?

ii) The difference between intention and cause.

Intentism concurs that an author cannot be fully cognizant of every influence and motivation. Partial intentionalist Intentists would parcel these mental functions with intention, however others would separate these influences as causes not intentions.

To an Intentist intentions can include the unconscious. Indeed, intentions invariably require unconscious performances. For example, in intending to read this sentence, each letter is not consciously linked to the others to formulate words. Rarely does a reader consciously turn the page of the book he or she is reading. A footballer intending to strike the ball will not normally be conscious of the various movements of his limbs needed to perform his expectation. Clearly, intentions can be unconscious.

World-renowned hand surgeon Dr. Brand writes of a bravura piano performance of a musical piece by such as Rubinstein. He begins by suggesting the pianist's intentions in playing by saying,' A good pianist controls his or her fingers independently...' The verb 'to control' suggests an intentional agent in the pianist and commending the agent as 'good' if these actions occur, again, suggest intention.

Brand then questions whether this agent is fully conscious of his actions:

From my own careful calculations, I know that some of the movements required, such as the powerful arpeggios in Moonlight's third movement, are simply too fast for the body to accomplish consciously. Nerve impulses do not travel with enough speed for the brain to sort out that the third finger has just lifted in time to order the fourth finger to strike the next key. Months of practice must pattern the brain to treat the movements as subconscious reflex actions – 'finger memory' musicians call it. (From 'Fearfully and Wonderfully Made.')

Furthermore, according to many Intentists there does seem to be a difference between intention and cause. A man falls in love with a girl and says, ' I love you.' He genuinely feels love towards her and expresses it. However, his lover exudes the same charisma as a previous girlfriend and has a smile that is particularly similar to his mother's. Both these are subconscious influences. These factors are possible causes of his expression, 'I love you' but the man intends to express his love for the girl and this is its fixed meaning, even if all the causes of his expression are not fully known to him. In other words, meaning is the outworking of intention, even if the audience understand the causes of the work more completely than the creator.

iii) Difficulties for the viewer to access the artist's intentions

One final argument against intentionalism to be addressed here is the difficulties that are present for a viewer to discover intention. Before addressing this,it is important to establish one point. It is considered by some that if intentions are hard to find, then the meaning of the work cannot be in the intention.

According to Intentists, this is either faulty thinking or manipulation. Before this question of difficulty is entertained, a decision must be made as to whether epistemologically intentions have an influence on a work's meaning. At this stage, how difficult the intention is to find is irrelevant. Only when a position is taken here should to approach to finding intention be looked at. In sum, it would be entirely consistent to believe firstly, that meaning is in the outworking of intention, and yet it is impossible to find sufficient evidence to objectively find that intention. Intentist argue that although it can be a challenge to discover an author's intentions, these difficulties are often exaggerated.

One difficulty often described as **Cartesian Dualism** is the separation between mind and body. The problem here is that the mind is not easily analysed. In essence, we can look at a work as it is in the world, but how can we look at a mind to discover its intention?

Intentists believe this difficulty is real but over-stated. Of course, it would be impossible to analyse any mind perfectly and to compound the issue, many artists/writers are dead. However, although it is impossible to omnisciently know the mind of another, it is possible to know adequately the **intention** of another.

iv) The mental baggage of the viewer.

Secondly, the baggage of the viewer may give him or her a bias in interpretation. No matter how hard the viewer looks to the artist's intention, their age, culture, sex, etc will influence their verdict. Again, this is certainly a difficulty and Intentists in general believe that the viewer with work can realize the most important obstacles for understanding. Intentists often relate the problem to a spiral where at the centre is the artist's intention. As the viewer becomes more aware of his mental baggage, he or she circles he intention getting closer to the intention. Although the viewer will never be able to discard his or her mental baggage entirely, Intentists would say that it is equally untrue that this means we can never get close enough to understand and engage with the intention.

v) The Hermeneutical Circle

The hermeneutical circle has become a great impasse in literary criticism. Put simply, the hermeneutical circle claims that one's understanding of the text as a whole is established by reference to the individual parts and one's understanding of each individual part by reference to the whole. In essence, this conundrum makes understanding of any text out of reach. There is much to be said for this analogy, and yet strikingly in the majority of instances everyday communication is successful.

Firstly, the degree of undecideables in any part of a text is exaggerated. In other words, there is a considerable number of interpretations that can invariably be ruled out. For example, the sentence' I am an artist' can be analysed a word at a time. 'I' is a pronoun; it is the first person and it must either be the subject or the object of the sentence (and consequently is not a verb, adjective or anything else.) 'Am' is a stative verb in the present simple first person. This suggests that 'I' is the subject of the sentence. 'An' is an indefinite article for countable nouns; therefore, the next word must be a noun or an adjective that describes who 'I am' is. Finally, the sentence concludes with the noun' artist.' Linguists have over the years parsed texts into separate units and this has on occasion obscured the fact that sentences and whole texts are interrelated and formed of collocations, patterns and chunks. These lexical chunks give clues to contexts an the whole and make the dilemma of the hermeneutical circle weaker.

An understanding of a text resembles a pendulum slowing down to stop in the centre. As the initial words of the text are read, comprehension of the text as a whole may change substantially with each unit, much like the pendulum. However, as the words are understood in context as in the example above, the wayward significances and associations are reduced, and the reader begins to understand the text more completely, finally resting, as the pendulum settles at a close understanding of the text.

The hermeneutical circle fails to give credit for the human mind's ability to collect and assimilate information. A simple example would be the game 'Twenty Questions' where the identity of a person or thing (i.e the whole) is discovered by understanding and gathering answers to individual closed questions. It is not considered an impossible game due to the hermeneutical circle, nor should it.

A final thought is this: There would be no reason for a narrative plot to succeed if the author cannot assume that the audience were able to build up the individual parts of the plot and mutually expect a certain conclusion.

In sum, perhaps a more accurate way of understanding this hermeneutical dilemma is to refer to a hermeneutical Spiral.

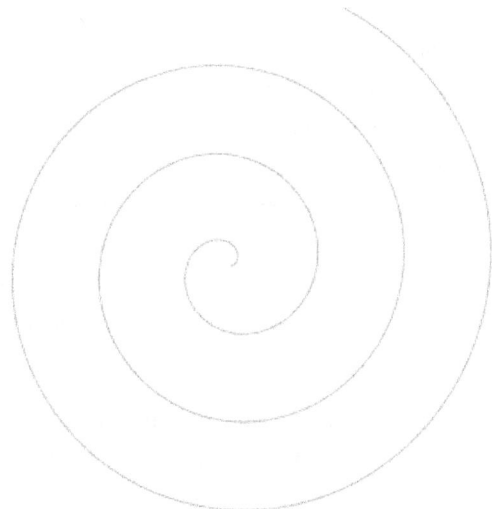

FIGURE 11 THE HERMENEUTICAL SPIRAL

In other words, it is not that the reader must continually go around and never reach an objective understanding. The reader can incrementally get closer to the text and the author's intention. Furthermore, Intentists would maintain that the intention and work's meaning is fixed in the centre. They would maintain that it is incorrect to say that a reader would read a text and be affected by it and to a degree changed and by being so the work to the reader is now a different text. This is significant because if this were the case then the viewer would be circling something that is permanently in flux and any fixed understanding would be impossible.

> It is undeniable that meanings unnoticed before and significances will be seen and appreciated in subsequent re-readings. However, these all originate in the reader as the meaning of the work is settled.

Philosopher Vanhoozer has named this ability to get closer as the **hermeneutical spiral**. Readers have certain baggage which means that the work is approached with certain prejudices. The work is interpreted in the light of these and initially the work may be understood with a great deal of personal significances and perhaps very little meaning. However, through study and close reading, these significances can be reduced and an understanding of the intention can be increased. There will always be remnant of significance and the work will never be understood omnisciently , but we can know it perfectly well for any real world use.

vi) Places to discover intention

If an artist can know his or her intention well enough; if the viewer can get let go of personal baggage to get sufficiently close to this intention, what are the appropriate sources to find intention?

Intention can be found in the artist's sketches, artist's notes, conversations with the artist, the oeuvre or the artist's body of work and the genre.

In sum, even though the audience can never know intentions omnisciently, they can be known in most cases truly.

> Note: A further argument against seeking intention from the author is that he or she might lie in interviews, sketches etc. However, no forgery cast doubt on the authentic.

vii) Multiple Intentions

An artist will never be governed by one intention. The artist will generally have a Meta-intention of their main idea and many micro-intentions. Furthermore, of course, intentions can change. The artist's final intention is to intend no more and at this point the whether the intentions have changed or not, all epistemological properties in the work are present.

To Intentists a good argument why this last intention to intend no more (and with it the possibility of changing meaning) is when death comes before this final intention. In this instance, the work is called 'unfinished' (for example, Beethoven's Unfinished symphony)

PART THREE: EXAMPLES OF INTENTIST WORK

i) Palimpsestism and the Creative Trail

If we now understand a little of Intentist theory, how is it manifest in art?

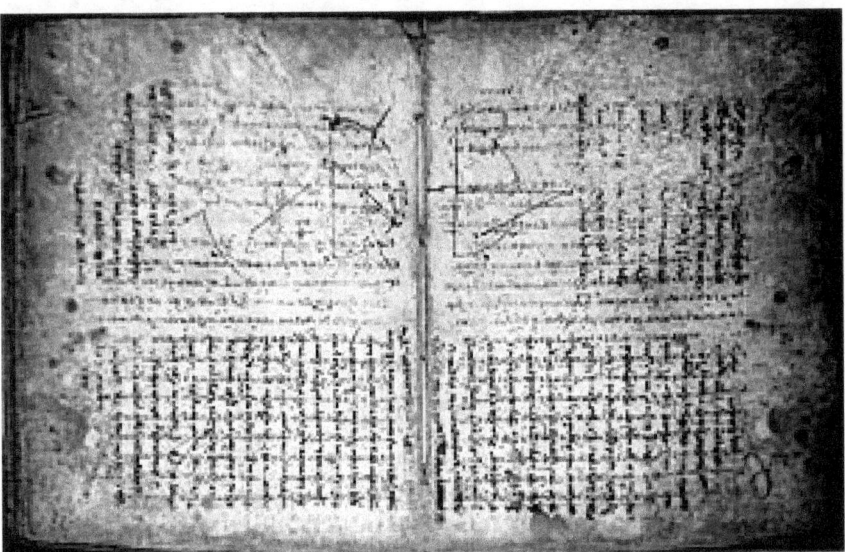

Firstly, Palimpsestism. A palimpsest is a manuscript that has been scraped off and reused. An example of this practice dates from Roman times when text would be written on wax-coated tablets that would be smoothed over and used again. Many Intentists are interested in this as sometimes the remnant of previous ideas can still be seen. These Intentists leave some of the editing process visible in the final work. Intentists have called this, 'the **creative trail.**'

Examples of Palimspsest Art

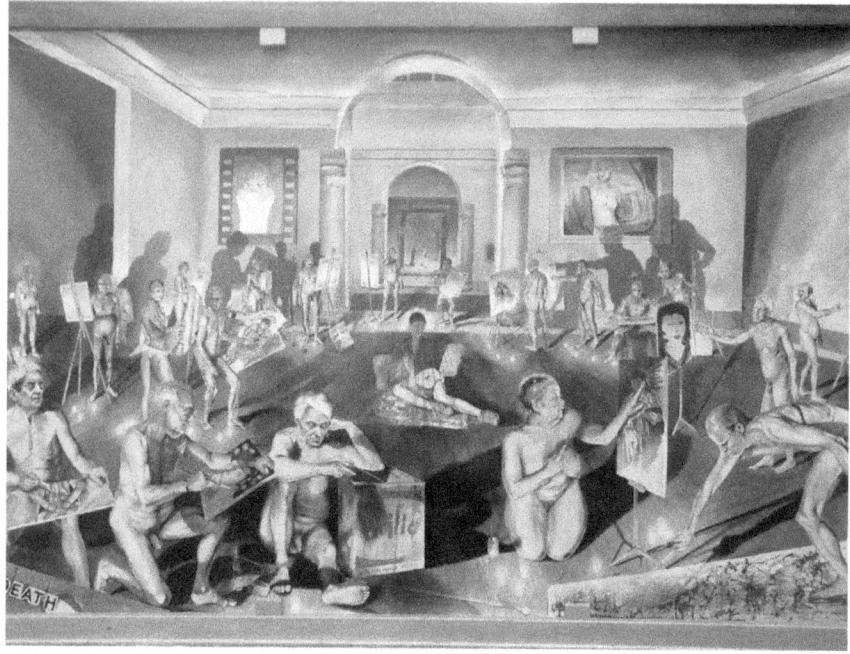

FIGURE 12 THE SCHOOL OF POSTMODERNISM BY VITTORIO PELOSI

The School of Postmodernism is a satire based on Raphael's, 'School of Athens,' in the Vatican

In the original, Raphael placed many of the most famous Greek thinkers and philosophers. In Pelosi's these have been replaced by figures that have been influential in postmodernism. The setting is a life drawing class, which is arguably the most objective art discipline. However, each artist's work is distorted through their own postmodern spectacles.

If you look closely you can see areas where earlier versions of a figure for example, are still visible.

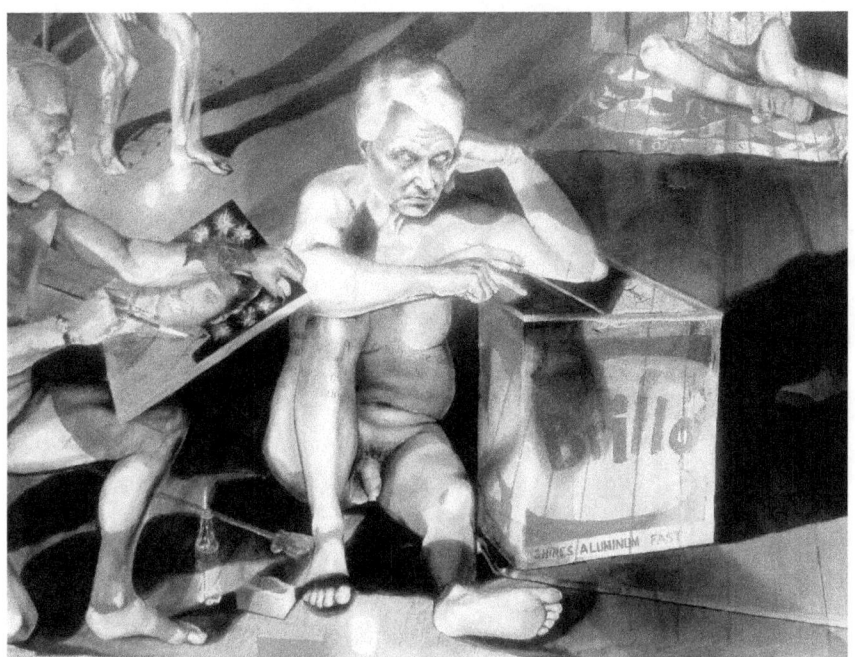

FIGURE 13 DETAIL FROM THE SCHOOL OF POSTMODERNISM

The Gamekeeper

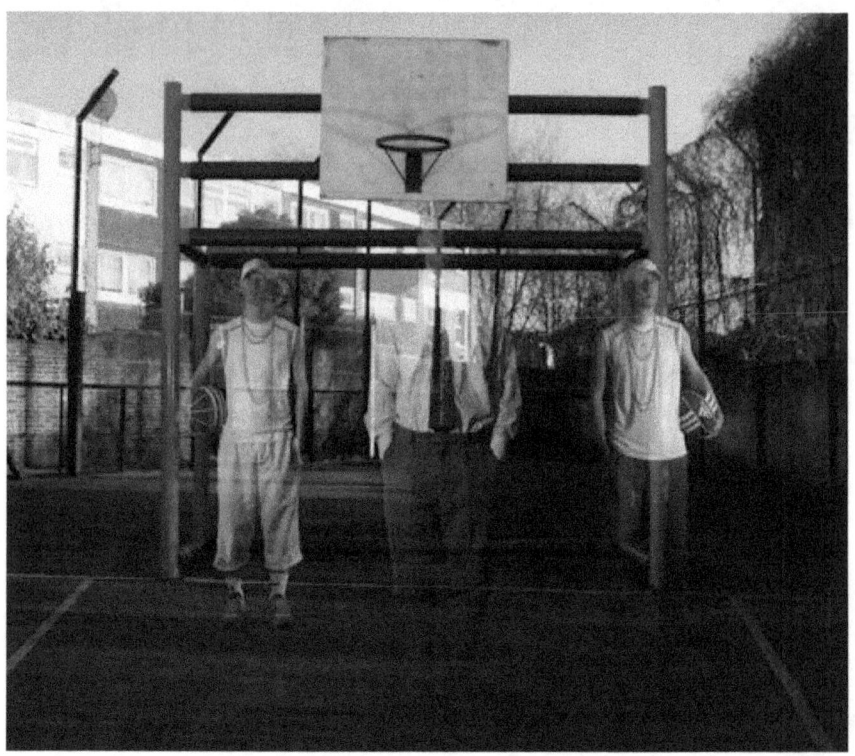

FIGURE 14 THE GAMEKEEPER BY CRAIG EDWARDS AND RHOD WALLS

This photograph illustrates Irony, puns, Palimpsestism and Creative Trail as it positions the figure in various possible locations in the finished work.

ii)   'Anarrative' art

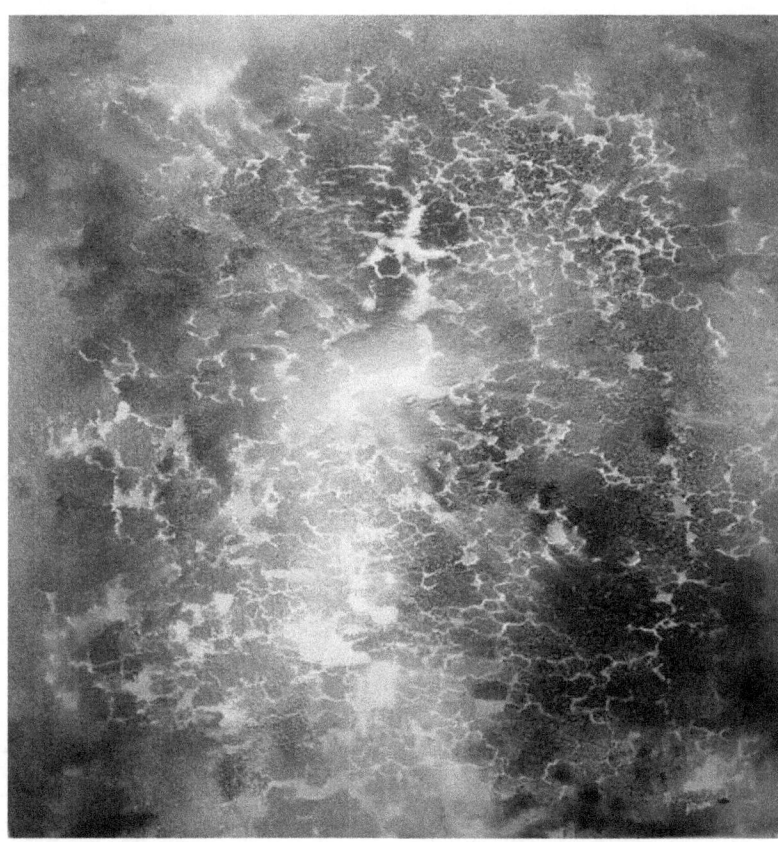

FIGURE 15 ANARRATIVE ART: HOPE AND HORROR BY GOVINDA SAH

Finally, as was stated previously, much art theory regarding the Death of the Artist finds it origin in literary theory. It is a claim of the Intentists that in certain fundamental areas this cross over is not valid. From Heidegger to Gadamer to Ricoeur, a basis for the hermeneutical theory of a 'fusion of horizons' is the relations between our narrative and the work's narrative. This argument was intended for texts where the author has a linear order expectation for the text since the viewer will normally start at the beginning and read letters sequentially until the end. However, this approach is not valid for the static arts. Most paintings and sculptures are 'anarrative' as viewers can approach the work in multiple orders. Therefore, this basis for ignoring the artist's intentions is no longer valid. An example in this book of an Intentist artist creating work to demonstrate anarrative is Govinda Sah.

iii)   Intentist Literature.

Grind

((Sitting on a train.

Weakened by the weather, (it's) gormless, overshadowed by
snippets from last night's dream,
Of love rejected.))

Slumped on a tube seat,
My head rattling against the casement window,
My stomach in knots,
(The power of 8,000 atoms)
(Still dreaming)
Having dreamt about a (girl) vision who left me six years
ago....
(Again).
And now, only waiting for tonight...
To wash away the lemon (traces) grinds of the night before.

By Gideon Parry 2009

In this work by Gideon Parry, the creative trail is still manifest in the word in parenthesis. Other Intentists have shown a similar approach by bracket the edited elements between commas.

iv)   Intentist Music

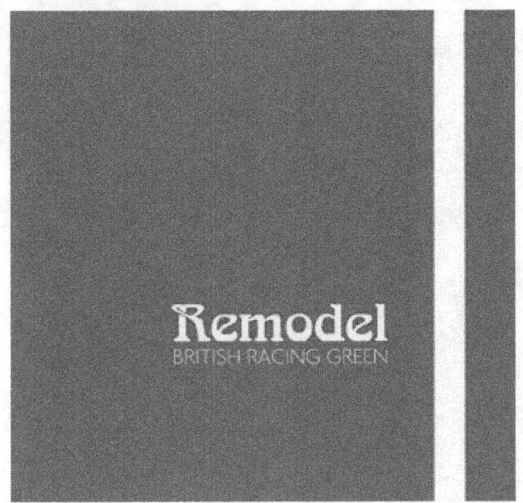

FIGURE 16 SINGLE SLEEVE COVER FOR 'THAT OBSCURE OBJECT CALLED DESIRE' BY REMODEL

Remodel was a very creative and popular band in the late noughties and 2010's. Their song 'That Obscure Object Called Desire' was recorded to demonstrate the band's intentional journey as the work changed and developed over time. In the recording, the earliest version can be heard in the right speaker, the latest in the left.

Intentism is an international art movement that includes artists, writers, actors, musicians and philosophers. We all share the *intentionalist* belief that the meaning of the work is the outworking of intention. We further maintain that in rejecting authorship and intention much creative work has become anemic and indifferent.
Consequently, our work celebrates intention by leaving a creative trail of the editorial process behind in the finished piece.